TABLE OF CONTENTS

Powerful Wings...5

The Body of the Bald Eagle...11

Bald Eagles and Their Nests...15

Eaglets...19

Unfair Criticism...26

An Endangered Bird...29

Ways to Save the Bald Eagle...35

Protecting the Bald Eagle...37

Words You Should Know...46

Index...47

POWERFUL WINGS

The bald eagle is found only in North America. It is one of the largest and most powerful hunting birds. Only the California condor is larger.

The bald eagle is called bald because its head is covered with white feathers. An old meaning of the word *bald* is "marked with white." There are white feathers on its tail, too.

On the ground the bald eagle looks clumsy. Its body may measure from 34 to 43 inches long. But in flight the bald eagle is beautiful.

The eagle's wings are long and broad. Its feathers are long and stiff. With a wingspan of up to 7-1/2 feet, adult bald eagles soar gracefully. With its long wingspan, it can glide a long distance. The air flows smoothly over the wing surface.

Bald eagle carries a branch back to its nest.

When the bird soars, the wing tips bend up.

These powerful wings help the birds to fly at speeds of 20 to 60 miles an hour. When the eagle

dives for prey, its speed
may reach 100 miles an
hour.

American bald eagles
can do rolls and loops like
airplanes doing tricks.

When a bald eagle flies,
its high, thin scream

Pair of adult bald eagles near their nest.
Can you tell which one is the female?

sounds like the creak of a
rusty hinge. It can be heard
over a long distance.

Female bald eagles are
bigger than the males.
Males weigh from 8 to 9
pounds. Females weigh 10
to 14 pounds.

THE BODY
OF THE BALD EAGLE

The bald eagle's head is very large. It is covered with white feathers. These white feathers extend down the neck. The large yellow eyes are on the sides of its head. Nevertheless, the bird can look straight ahead.

Eagles have the best eyesight of any bird. Their

eyesight may be five or
six times better than ours.

Bald eagles are birds of
prey.

While flying high in the
air, they can spot their
prey. However, they usually
hunt much closer to the
water or ground.

Their bright yellow beaks
are large and strong. The
sharp hook at the tip helps
them tear up their food.

The bald eagle's feet
and legs are strong. The
bright yellow feet have

The bald eagle's powerful beak and
sharp talons are used as weapons.

Bald eagle carries a fish in its talons.

long, curved talons. The birds kill with these talons. Often they carry their food back to their nests. Young chicks, or eaglets, in the nest eagerly wait for their parents to bring them food.

BALD EAGLES AND THEIR NESTS

The American bald eagle mates for life. However, if one mate dies, the other will find a new mate.

The birds build their nests in the tops of tall trees or on high cliffs. An eagle's nest is called an aerie. The nest may be built 10 to 150 feet above the ground. The pair builds the nest of twigs, moss, grass, pine needles, and feathers. The nest may be six feet wide and six feet deep.

The same aerie is used by the pair for ten years or longer. Through the years the eagles make the aerie larger. Some nests become twenty feet wide and nine feet deep. The eagles often bring fresh leaves, grass, and branches to make the aerie larger.

A pair of adult eagles repair their nest.

Nests are usually built
near rivers or wetlands.
There the birds can catch
fish. In some places where
the birds catch rodents,
the nests may be built on
mountain ledges.

Eagles migrate. Many spend
the winter along the
Mississippi and Illinois rivers.
Others go to Florida, Texas,
or Louisiana. Bald eagles are
found throughout the United
States. The largest number nest
in Alaska.

EAGLETS

Females usually lay two eggs each year. In the northern United States and Canada they lay their eggs in March. Bald eagles in Florida lay their eggs from September to January.

The eggs are three inches long and two inches across. The female sits on the

eggs for most of the forty
days, keeping them warm
before they hatch. Her mate
brings her food. Sometimes
he takes a turn sitting
on the eggs.

When the eaglet is
ready to hatch, it pecks at
the shell with its egg
tooth. The egg tooth is a
small, pointed tooth on the
tip of the eaglet's beak. It

Eaglet in its nest

may take four hours before
the eaglet can break out
of its egg. The special egg
tooth drops off after the
eaglet has left its shell.

21

The eaglets hatch with their eyes open. They are very weak and helpless. They are covered with a grayish white down. In two or three weeks this is replaced with a thicker gray down. Feathers

Can you see what is left of this eaglet's gray down?

These eaglets are nine weeks old.

appear when the young
are four or five weeks old.

Usually the eggs hatch
two or three days apart.
The second bird to hatch
may be smaller and
weaker. Often it cannot

compete for the food the parents bring and dies.

When they are seventy to seventy-five days old, the eaglets grow their flight feathers, or fledge. The new feathers are strong enough to permit them to fly.

Until they are four or five years old, the young eagles have dark brown feathers. White patches are found under the wings and on other parts of their bodies. Young bald eagles

This young bald eagle does not yet have the white head, neck, and tail feathers of the adult.

may be mistaken for other kinds of eagles. But as they mature, the young bald eagles get their white head, neck, and tail feathers. The rest of their feathers are dark brown, almost black.

UNFAIR CRITICISM

Many people used to think bald eagles killed chickens or baby farm animals. Actually this happens rarely. Bald eagles prefer fish, especially catfish. They eat wild ducks and other game birds. Squirrels and other rodents are also

This young bald eagle (left), feeding on a dead salmon, was suddenly attacked by an adult eagle trying to steal the salmon.

included in their diet. Small fish are eaten on the wing. Larger fish and small animals are brought back to the nest.

27

Bald eagle feeding on a dead deer

Animals killed on the roadside are often carried off and eaten by eagles. The dead animals are called carrion. In some states, the bald eagle's chief diet may be carrion.

AN ENDANGERED BIRD

Once there may have been 75,000 bald eagles. By 1971 there were less than 2,500. There were many reasons why this happened. The eagles' natural habitats, or homes, had been lost when towns were built in nesting areas. Hunters shot many eagles for sport.

Farmers and ranchers thought the eagles killed chickens, lambs, and other farm animals. They shot the birds. Other people robbed eggs from eagle nests. So the eagle population declined.

For many years, a chemical called DDT was sprayed on crops and in swamps. The DDT was used to kill harmful insects that ate crops or spread diseases.

Crop duster spraying chemicals on a corn crop.

At first DDT was thought
to be nontoxic, or safe to
use. Following World War II,
it was used on crops in
the United States and
throughout the world.

But DDT was not safe. It did not break down, or become harmless, quickly. It washed down into rivers and lakes. Water plants and animals absorbed the DDT. Fish ate these plants and animals. The eagles, in turn, ate the fish.

The DDT prevented the eagles from making strong eggshells. Because of DDT, the eagles' eggs had thin shells. They were easily crushed. Fewer and fewer eggs hatched. Bird watchers counted very few eaglets. Other fish-eating birds were also affected.

The eagles faced another problem. Hunters used lead shot or pellets

in their guns. Many ducks and Canada geese that were wounded or killed were eaten by the eagles. When they ate these waterfowl, they developed lead poisoning.

People were afraid the American bald eagle might become extinct.

WAYS TO SAVE
THE BALD EAGLE

In 1940 the U.S.
Congress made it illegal to
shoot eagles or to take
their eggs from their nests.
Then in 1972 the use of
DDT, which endangered
many birds, was banned.

In regions where bald
eagles and waterfowl are
hunted, lead pellets are
banned. Hunters must use
steel (nontoxic) shot in

Today laws protect the bald eagles and their nesting grounds (left).

their guns in many
counties in Illinois along
the Mississippi and Illinois
rivers. Soon there may be
a total ban on the use of
lead shot or pellets.

PROTECTING
THE BALD EAGLE

The bald eagle has a life span of twenty to thirty years in the wild. It may become fifty years old in captivity, where it is protected. Only about fifty percent of the eaglets reach adulthood.

It is important to protect these magnificent birds in the wild. Over two hundred

Can you see
what this eagle
caught
for dinner?

national wildlife refuges
now have eagles. Some
refuges were established
especially for the eagles.
Federal and state agencies,
as well as conservation
groups, assist in the
program.

The U.S. Fish and Wildlife Service runs a research center where captive breeding is conducted. Most of the adult eagles in the breeding program have been injured. They could not survive in the wild. They nest at the research center.

Scientists carefully remove the eggs from the nests. The eggs are incubated artificially. When

Bird handler working with a trained bald eagle

the eaglets are three
weeks old, they are placed
in the nests of eagles in
the wild. More than
seventy healthy eaglets
have been raised. The
center has been enlarged
so the program can expand.

Forty-three states list the bald eagle as an endangered species. Five more states list it as threatened. The Bald Eagle Protection Act of 1940 provides for heavy fines and prison terms for people who interfere with the bald eagle in any way.

Bald eagle drys its wings in the sun.

In the early 1960s there were only five hundred nesting pairs in the "lower forty-eight states." By 1985 the number had risen to 1,700 breeding pairs. Alaska alone has 3,300 pairs.

Since 1782 the bald

The Great Seal of the United States of America

eagle has been the national emblem of the United States. The Great Seal of the United States, adopted in 1789, bears the picture of the bald eagle.

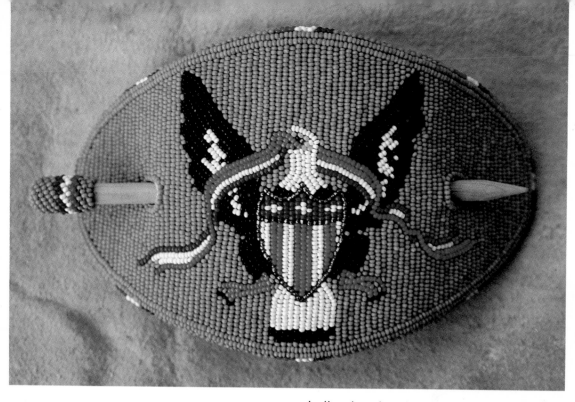

Indian beadwork showing the bald eagle

For over two hundred years the bald eagle has been a symbol of the United States. Today hundreds of people are working to save the bald eagle from extinction.

WORDS YOU SHOULD KNOW

aerie(EE • ree) — an eagle's nest

bird of prey(BERD UV PRAY) — a bird that catches and eats other animals

captive(KAP • tihv) — not free; held in a cage

carrion(KAIR • ee • yun) — dead animals that are found and eaten by other animals

eaglet(EE • glit) — a baby eagle

emblem(EM • blum) — something that stands for an idea

endangered(en • DAYN • jerd) — in danger of dying out

extinct(ex • TINKT) — no longer living

fledge(FLEJ) — to grow the feathers needed to fly

habitat(HAB • ih • tat) — the place where an animal usually is found

incubate(ING • kyoo • bait) — to keep eggs warm until they hatch

nontoxic(non • TAHX • ik) — not poisonous; not harmful

prey(PRAY) — an animal that is killed and eaten by another animal

refuge(REF • yooj) — a safe place where animals can live without being harmed by people

rodent(ROH • dint) — small furry animals such as squirrels and mice

symbol(SIM • bul) — a thing that stands for something else

talons(TAL • unz) — long, sharp claws

INDEX

adults, 6, 24, 25, 39
aerie, 15, 16
Alaska, 18, 42
American bald eagle, 5, 8, 15
Bald Eagle Protection Act, 41
beaks, 13, 20
body, 11-14
breeding, 39-40, 42
California condor, 5
Canada, 19
Canada geese, 34
captivity, 37, 39-40
carrion, 28
catfish, 26
color, feather, 5, 11, 22, 24, 25
Congress, U.S., 35
DDT, 30-32
diet, 26-28
down, 22
ducks, 26, 34
eaglets, 14, 19-25, 33, 37
egg robbers, 30, 35
eggs, 19, 20-21, 32, 39-40
egg tooth, 20-21
emblem, national, 43
endangered bird, 29-34, 35, 41
extinction, 34, 45
eyes, 11, 22
eyesight, 11-12
farm animals, 30
feathers, 5, 6, 11, 22-23, 24, 25

feet, 13-14
females, 9, 19
fish, 17, 26, 27, 32, 33
fledge, 24
Florida, 18, 19
flying, 6, 8, 11, 24
food, 13, 14, 20, 26-27
Great Seal of the United States, 43
growth, 20-25
hatching, 20, 21, 22, 23, 33
head, 5, 11, 25
hook, 13
hunters, 29, 33, 35-36
hunting bird, 5, 12
Illinois, 18, 36
incubation, 39
killers, 14, 26, 30
lead poisoning, 34
lead shot, 33-34, 35-36
legs, 13
life span, 37
Louisiana, 18
mating, 15
migration, 18
Mississippi, 18, 36
mountain ledges, 17
national emblem, 43
neck feathers, 11, 25
nesting areas, 29
nests, 15-17

North America, 5

poisoning, chemical 30-33, 33-34

population, 29, 30, 40, 42

prey, 8, 12

protection, 37-41, 45

ranchers, 30

refuges, 37-38

research center, 39-40

rivers, 17, 18

rodents, 17, 27

scientists, 39-40

scream, 8-9

shot, lead, 33-34

sight, 11-12

size, 5, 6, 9

speed, 7, 8

squirrels, 26

tail feathers, 5, 25

talons, 13-14

Texas, 18

tooth, egg, 20

United States, 18, 19, 31, 43

U.S. Fish and Wildlife Service, 39

weight, 9

wetlands, 17

wildlife refuges, 38

wings, 6, 7, 24

World War II, 31

young, 14, 19-25

About the Author

Emilie Utteg Lepthien earned a BS and MS Degree and a certificate in school administration from Northwestern University. She has worked as an upper grade science and social studies teacher supervisor and a principal of an elementary and upper grade center for twenty years. Ms. Lepthien also has written and narrated science and social studies scripts for the Radio Council of the Chicago Board of Education.

Ms. Lepthien was awarded the American Educator's Medal by Freedoms Foundation. She is a member of the Delta Kappa Gamma Society International, Chicago Principals Association and life member of the NEA. She has been a co-author of primary social studies texts for Rand, McNally and Co. and an educational consultant for Encyclopaedia Britannica Films.